What people are saying about BORICUA PASSPORT

J.L. Torres' poems draw a line in the sand from the blue green crystal clear agua buenas of Puerto Rico to the blue salsa funk of the Boogie Down. He takes us Salsa dancing through the rhythms of his words, their rich, visceral, viscous texture and specificity to the deep down soulscapes of each image-driven memory of what it means to be a Rican constructing a reality from the belly of that which devours dreams. You don't need a passport to be transported to the world(s) in the words of Torres' verse—just your heart and head and an imagination scopic and distended as the universe.

—Tony Medina, Poet, Professor, Activist
author of *Broke Baroque* (2leaf Press, 2013)

If you are a Boricua from the Bronx, you will delight in a multisensory landscape that takes back a beauty often obscured by the hard times, and denied by those who know the Bronx only as an ugly rumor. You will recognize the sights and aromas; you will know the people. Some poems might make you angry, others will make you recall your own experiences. Those who fear and revile our beautiful and complex Bronx, might want to hop a train after reading this collection.

—Magadalena Gomez, Poet and Playwright
Co-founder and Artisitic Director of Teatro V!da

I bless J.L.Torres for writing *Boricua Passport.* This collection of poems took me back to my old neighborhood. Thank you Torres for writing about the bodega and cuchifritos. I can hear the plane in "Departures" stumbling in the air pass the St. Mary's Projects and crashing in the nearby park. Torres' poetry kisses my ears and lips. To be Puerto Rican is to write from the center of love embracing the complexity of identity. To be Nuyorican is to continue moving and transforming the world. Every imagination requires a passport. Torres stamps my heart with words.

—E. Ethelbert Miller
Award-winning Poet and Literary Activist

Like his mother, who wrote her history on "every grain of rice,"

Torres marks the story of his journey through cultural displacement with these poems. The ever shifting notion of "home," the ever evolving narrative of identity, emerge from poems like Doña Vista, Legacy, To White Editors, and Letrina.

—Naomi Ayala
author of *Calling Home: Praise Songs and Incantations*

Against Disneyfied caricatures of Boricua mobility, J.L.Torres proposes a mobilization of memory, a mapping of his/our varied turfs: the "asphalt borderlands" of the South Bronx, the "home(is)land" of Puerto Rico, far upstate and its "Carajo counties," and most of all the unincorporated territories of the soul and body. This is not your abuelita's poetry, except that it is--tu sabes? In the spirit of Rev. Pedro Pietri, Torres seeks out the "location of this nothingness" where we all scrawl our own passports in in(di)visible ink. Watch /here/ and /there/ blur! This /Boricua Passport/ has your name.

—Urayoán Noel, Poet and Scholar
author of *Los días porosos* (Catafixia Editorial, 2012)

In *Boricua Passport,* J.L. Torres guides his reader through a morphing homeland; from paradise to housing projects, from sand-filled island beaches to summer tarred city rooftops. The scape of the land he calls home mutates before your eyes. Torres' homeland is found in his suffering mother, his place of birth is the person who is his father. His readers experience the transformation of a people. Grief caused by family separation, the horrific life of slavery, the brutal working life in the fields, the alienation of one's identity, is transformed anew with vitality and pride. In the end, we arrive back home to our abuela and the bata. In the end, the final homeland is the one found in one another for in our mutual dance lies the resurrection of our nation.

—Nancy Mercado, PhD
Writer, Editor

BORICUA PASSPORT

POEMS BY J.L. TORRES

NUYORICAN WORLD SERIES

NEW YORK

www.2leafpress.org

2LEAF★PRESS

P.O. Box 4378
Grand Central Station
New York, New York 10163-4378
editor@2leafpress.org
www.2leafpress.org

2LEAF PRESS
is an imprint of the
Intercultural Alliance of Artists & Scholars, Inc. (IAAS),
a NY-based nonprofit 501(c)(3) organization that promotes
multicultural literature and literacy.
www.theiaas.org

Cover art: and design Richard "Vagabond" Beaumont
Book design and layout: Gabrielle David

Library of Congress Control Number: 2013954040
ISBN-13: 978-1-940939-19-3 (Paperback)
ISBN-13: 978-1-940939-20-9 (eBook)

10 9 8 7 6 5 4 3 2 1

Published in the United States of America

First Edition | First Printing

The Publisher wishes to thank Vagabond Beaumont for the wonderful cover art, with special thanks to Carolina Fung Feng for providing the "Third Eye" with her great copy editing.

2LEAF PRESS trade distribution is handled by University of Chicago Press / Chicago Distribution Center (www.press.uchicago.edu) 773.702.7010. Titles are also available for corporate, premium, and special sales. Please direct inquiries to the UCP Sales Department, 773.702.7248.

For Lee, my lady in red.

CONTENTS

PART I: THERE / ACÁ

PART II: ALLÁ / HERE

ACKNOWLEDGMENTS

THESE POEMS HAVE APPEARED in the following publications, sometimes in earlier versions. I thank the editors, to whom grateful acknowledgment is made:

African Voices: "Carimbo"

The Americas Review: "Walking the Ghetto with Miguel and Piri"

Anthology: "Abuela"

Bilingual Review: "BiWays," "Letrina," "Danny," "Exotic Cuisine," "To White Editors"

Blue Collar Review: "Madre(Patria), "Blood"

The Connecticut Review: "Lilo Returns"

Crab Orchard Review: "The Crux," "Salsa Dancing"

The Denver Quarterly: "Bronx Aubade"

Epicenter: "The Sanctity of Cuchifritos"

Palabra: "Speechless in Carajo County"

Puerto del Sol: "Hoops"

Revista Cayey: "Father(Land)"

Revista Interamericana/Interamerican Review: "Huracan," "Pitiyanqui"

Santa Clara Review: "A Trail in the Rain Forest"

Spout: "Diasporican Blues"

Struggle: "America Ain't No Disneyland," "Doña Vista Talks Suitcases," "Flying Beach Chairs."

Suisun Valley Review: "Rooftop"

Timbooktu: " Carimbo"

Tulane Review: "Salsa Dancing"

Valparaiso Poetry Review: "Legacy"

Thanks to Charles Touhey and Alice Green for giving me the opportunity to stay at the Paden Institute's cottage to work on this collection. I would also like to thank Michael Carrino and E. Ethelbert Miller for their valuable feedback on earlier versions of the manuscript and for their encouragement and support. Special thanks to Naomi Ayala, Magdalena Gómez, Nancy Mercado, Tony Medina, and Urayoán Noel for reading this collection and commenting on it. Como siempre, thanks to my wife, Lee, and sons, Alex and Julian, for their love and support. Many thanks to those poets whose work inspires me, whose words enrich my life and save me from "dying miserably every day."★

INTRODUCTION
Visa to a Puerto Rican Mindscape

PUERTO RICO HAS BEEN A COLONY of the United States for over a century, but few Americans know much about the Island and its people. In fact, most Americans, and even some Puerto Ricans, do not comprehend that the island is indeed a colony. The island, at the historical moment when it was struggling for its independence from Spain, was invaded in a deliberate, aggressive imperialist move to grab it and convert it to an American military outpost and geopolitical stronghold in the Caribbean. Puerto Rico, like the Philippines (which the U.S. also invaded during the war and attempted to colonize but failed against a strong resistance), had little to do with the Maine or Cuba for that matter—the "official" reasons often cited for the Spanish-American War that led to the island's colonial bondage. Despite having a modicum of internal governance, the political reality of the island and its people remains one of continued colonization. The United Nations has so deemed on various occasions.

You would think that the least the United States could do—after colonizing over eight million people and their homeland for that long—is to get some of the basic facts about us right. Like: we have been citizens of the United States since 1917. Consider the xenophobic backlash against Marc Anthony singing "God Bless America" recently at a baseball All-Star Game. (Personally, I don't know how many times I've been asked if I have a green card). Some do not know that Puerto Rico is indeed an island and requires traveling by air and not ground transportation. Or that Puerto Rico cannot vote for President, and we have no representation with vote in the U.S. Congress, although our men and women have served in the various branches of the armed forces and died in American wars. That the island uses the U.S. and not Puerto Rican dollar as its currency (I've been asked if I wanted a check cut by the University of Puerto Rico in U.S. dollars). That tacos and tamales, and any other Mexican food, are not part of Puerto Rican traditional cuisine. That Puerto Ricans must travel with a U.S. passport because as a colony we do not have one of our own (thus the ironic title of this collection). And the list goes on.

I supposed such ignorance is the privilege of the colonizer and those of us struggling with the colonial condition are expected to deal with it. But this type of cluelessness and the annoying questions and comments it engenders doesn't come close to how colonization marks one's mind and spirit. After more than half a century living between the United States and Puerto Rico, I can honestly say that I don't belong to or in either one. The uncertainty that sensibility brings, the sensation of rootlessness, of continual estrangement, of lacking an integral slice of one's identity and history, is an omnipresent absence. It is a vexing, problematic and restless state of affairs for me. For how do I know what my identity can or should be if gaps are missing, forever gone; historical and cultural pieces essential for me to put the identity puzzle together. To utter either "I'm Puerto Rican" or "I'm an American" always seems hollow to me. In either case I speak the words for a given context and purpose and yet the words still feel empty of real contextual significance. Like many Nuyoricans I have learned to shift cultural gears depending on the various situations I confront. To construct and live an awkward, uncomfortable, and tenuous hybrid existence.

Individuals grounded by history, by a long line of geographically-rooted ancestry probably cannot comprehend this feeling. Those individuals are most likely the same ones who arrogantly inform me that in this postmodern, postcolonial world all this talk of identity formation is unwarranted and meaningless. (Postcolonial? We're still working on colonial.) Gayatri Spivak's work on "strategic essentialism" serves as a critical response to that type of thinking. I hope that this collection serves as literary testimony that for me, and many other Puerto Ricans, a search for identity—even one shattered—is not a meaningless pursuit. The striving to find the broken pieces and to reconstruct them in some form that offers collective agency and hope is at the heart of any colonized people's struggle for freedom.

These poems attempt to evoke the complex inbetweeness that represents the contemporary Puerto Rican condition as filtered through the prism of my life experience. The collection contains a variety of forms, a good smattering of narrative poems but also includes the lyric, a form often neglected and dismissed by poets who write on political themes and, for some reason, think that these themes can only be advanced through narrative poetics. I've tried to integrate different voices and registers—Bakhtin is always lurking in the back of my mind. Many of these poems are grounded in place, because my sense of rootlessness and restlessness often compel me to seek meaning in physical space.

Ultimately, I hope that this collection may serve as a bridge to understanding Puerto Rico, its culture and history. I'm hoping that it also offers some insights into the colonial existence that most Puerto Ricans live. But most importantly, I hope they provoke and engage you as they bring you some aesthetic pleasure.⊛

—J.L. Torres
Plattsburgh, NY, 2013

PART I: THERE / ACÁ

A good traveler is one who does not know
where he is going to,
and a perfect traveler does not know
where he came from.

—Lin Yutang, *The Importance of Living*

Huracán

The Taíno god
unleashes
the bronze furies

headless spirits
roaming through
darkness lost
they ride the howling
tide

inside
petrified shadows
wait
humbled
before
the rain speckled
door

Boricua Passport

A retired revolutionary
constructed one out of cardboard,
pasted a Taíno symbol meaning
"pass into the mist."
Like a confused tourist at the airport,
he asked questions no one answered.

The "Rich Port" without a pass,
no pasa—que pasa? Quien pasa?
No Puerto Rican passes.

'Cause there's no passport for boundaries
set in topographic mindscapes.
No sovereignty granted for indignation
over Madonna humping the PR flag,
Kramer burning it in Seinfeld.
None, in Olympian pride scanning
the "Boricuas in Sports" page,
or Puerto Rican beauty queen
wearing Miss Universe crown.
Don't expect pass-ports for eating
Cuchifritos in the Bronx, wearing
coquí jewelry, displaying
"Kiss me I'm Puerto Rican"
buttons at the annual parade.

We have a notion, not a nation,
desplegaos presenting insular
credentials of patria, undocumented
visas to inertia.

But what we need is a passport
            to our broken
                        memory.

Flying Beach Chairs

In the black and white photo
men sit on beach chairs,
on an army transport plane.
Traveling boricuas, not vacationing
by the oceanside, tanning themselves.
They're leaving the beaches of their
homeland to pick the fruit for
gringo tables. They're not sipping
a fría by Luquillo, a good thing
because nothing holds the flimsy chairs;
the flyers need not worry
about spilling cocktails,
or forgetting to put back their trays.

Will they ever see a beach chair
in America? In between winters
when the sunny days will find them
soaking rays under a watchful eye,
unable to take a dip in the ocean,
now a distant memory.
Their fingers snap the fruit from trees,
not at a cabana boy who looks like them,
to fetch a cool drink 'cause
their dry throats have lost the ability
to utter sounds amid their laboring silence.
The upshot is now they have ample time
to think about finding a better travel agent,
one who can get a better package deal
that does not include flying beach chairs.

Blood

In memory of Don Efrain

You came to America, arms extended,
sweat running down muscular grooves,
waiting for the bundle to drop.
In Wisconsin, you picked fruit.
In Chicago and New York, you labored
in factories, never missed a day.

Never complained, even when the new boss
gave your foreman job to an anglo,
on the same day you moved
into the better neighborhood.
You celebrated with the kids, anyway,
found another job, never missed a day,
never late, never sick until you retired.

The blood that once gave your body power,
destroyed it when you stopped for rest.
But we would rather remember how your blood
flowed through your veins, stronger and sweeter
than the coffee you drank, a transfusion of will
for those who bleed a little every day.

Doña Vista

South Bronx Oracle.
Virgen de las ventanas
perched on the fifth floor.
Her kabuki frowned face framed
by opened window, caged against
the steel safety guard.
Wiry hair dancing like medusa's locks.
Sentinel elbows and arms sphinxing
her stout body.
Doña Vista sees.
Doña Vista speaks.
Her eyes touch all —
her voice reaches
the asphalt borderlands.

Hoops

A dull whack
silenced their trash, halted
the squeaky stutter steps.

The man fell
like a wobbly steer.
The other stood over him
machete in hand
until the last curse
spewed from his mouth.

The crowd watching
dispersed like vultures
from road kill,
when the woman fell
to her knees
and scooped his head.
She howled
at the blood
curling toward the curb.

Twirling the basketball,
the teen wondered
if this guy
would get up.

Fingering his chain,
another player noticed
her chest, tagged red.

The cops'll come,
someone finally said,
and the ball found the cement,
the bouncing again as steady
as a heartbeat.

Ghost

You run up the stairs,
your eyes glowing,
your heart dancing,
and stop in your tracks.

There,
on the landing,
he slumps, pale-skinned,
dark crescents cradling eyes
looking upwards, supplicant,
a figure out of El Greco's mind.

You shuffle around him,
the stink of urine,
soiled pants making
you want to puke.
The dangling needle,
making you want to stare.

You enter the apartment,
embraced by smells cooking
on the stove, and escape
to your room.
Your mother yells:
"Did you see a ghost?"

You drop on the bed,
forgetting the news
that had excited you.
The principal shaking your hand,
in front of the whole school,
for getting the highest
midterm grades.

Rooftop

During summer, when it's tar beach,
we spread towels, tune in Radio Seduction.
The beer drops like monsoon rain,
& car honking dissolves like waves into sand.
Buildings become tree shade, & you swear
the air's salty sweet, like taffy.

Other days, the door creaks open
onto a bordered cloud, the sky's
your ceiling, one rung closer
to heaven, Concrete Nirvana;
where yerba floats
like incense at a séance,
and prayers lunge for the kicks
that landed a perfect sidewalk somersault.

At night, the skyline tinkles
like cheap disco lights.
From some cloistered corner,
a capella voices echo;
timbales and trumpets duel;
a fiery sax spits out notes,
& someone always looks up to say:
if we could only see the stars.

The Sanctity of Cuchifritos

Mecca called and I followed.
The cuchifrito stand on 116th,
the temple of cuchifritos, the one
by the defunct Cosmo Theater.

I step up to the altar
to take the bombilla food
along with other worshippers.

> Alcapurrias, morcillas, cuajito
> Relleno de papa, empanadas,
> Chicharrones de cerdo, amen

The smells anoint you,
the respectful quiet reserved
for the sacred surrounds you.
Puerto Rican food for the soul.

The 24 hour shrine welcomes all pilgrims.
The summer days were best,
when after discotequing,
your sexual hunger still on fire,
you sated your stomach's aching,
in that place alive with talk and spirit.
And you left able to confront the trek
back home on the Pelham Express.

But on a frigid winter's day
when the snow fell
sad and still over the food,
a junkie mused
about the heavy eating going down,
so serious to silence Puerto Ricans.
We all laughed in communion
and the cold could not touch us.

Salsa Dancing

I never learned the intricacies
of salsa dancing, or the syncopated
mincing cha-cha steps.
But my body drew power
from notes quivering
from the tumbao,
the beat fluttering over
my skin, a lover's breath.

With the lights flashing,
history rolled like a newsreel.
And I was *there* bending knees,
hips shaking, battling the drums;
a flute solo filled the ballroom,
danzas during tiempo muerto;
trumpets heralded the cafetales bursting
with harvest, the coro narrated
the struggles across an ocean
as feet shuffled over wood
to rhythms of clinking chain.

The heritage embraced me,
the lost relative
who could not dance, witnessing
boricuas work the floor
in ways alien to our past.
Flaunting fashion at the expense of food.
Vanity creating islands
on a restless sea of rumberos.

With every snort we drifted
to oblivion, every English word
uttered split our tongues.
Every drink abetted our amnesia.
Lotus-eaters with rhythm

sliding across the floor,
lost but beautiful to watch.
Barrio streets appeared distant;
in the dark all bruises disappeared.
The loud music drowned out
slashing words that bleed families thin.
Unopened bills on rickety tables,
mice hunting under a moon-hungry night,
and garbage trucks wailed the start
of another lay-a-way day.

My feet straddled
a moment of recognition,
and I hated the scene.
But as I glowed in the comfort
of rhythms spinning my head,
melodies ripping my chest,
I spotted a couple dancing,
sensual like fog floating
across the cordillera—and I, too,
am up, stumbling and faltering,
but dancing, dancing.

Doña Vista: Con Lo Que Cuenta América

Look at him so happy with his cute knapsack with dem ugly
cartoon characters. That young they get excited about buy-
ing pencils, you know? Go to school like it's an adventure.
But most end up like that one there. Hundred dollar jersey,
lujo sneakers—cost more than what I spend on groceries a
week. Pants showing crack of his ass, pant legs sweeping
the streets—Sanitation should pay him. Tilted cap make his
head look crooked. Buzzheads—that's what they are. Nothing
upstairs but flies—Everything baggy—where they gonna work
lookin' like that? Can't understand what they're saying half the
time. A freakin' cell phone glued to their heads—La nueva gen-
eración—con lo que cuenta América. Glad I'll be dead before
they in charge.

Sanctuary

Within four tight walls, a radio sputtered
music from the street sirens who beckoned:
"Smash yourself against the curb."
I read hours in that bedroom, barricaded
against South Bronx shadows.
From there, I saw colors and sunlight,
the shape of things, while I stared
at hollow faces outside,
reached for their ghostly hands.

Now, in this carrel I prepare
to talk about colors, sunlight
and the shape of things.
Few will listen.
My eyes glaze through the window
to lusty lawns and houses
with unlocked doors and U.S. flags.
The light above dims the room cold.
I return to my work.
Spirits gather to pray.
En coro, they chant Qué Viva Shangó.

Hidden White People

On rare moments
they scurried from their apartments,
their paleness crashing against
brown bodies crowding a street
they once inhabited, when America
seemed simpler and the others
had not yet migrated like birds
escaping the changing season.
They scuttled to church,
to buy items at the supermarket,
never the bodega,
then returned to their caves.
But they didn't come out that time
Pedro flew out the 3rd floor window.
Didn't run out to ogle the spot
tainted with blood and jellied flesh.
They looked from above
at the hordes below wrapping
the shaking body in foreign words.
Pedro laying on his face, the whispers
bubbling from purple lips unable
to reach them behind their
thick white curtains.

J.J. KoolRican Raps
"America Ain't No Disneyland"

Heard you took the pilgrimage to Mousetown.
Now you talking 'bout bringing that star down
attach it to the flag, let's take a stand.
Yo, America ain't no Disneyland.

Don't be thinkin' with your teeny pinga.
Stop talkin' caca about some gringas
gettin' you hard for a jíbaro state.
Hell no, no way we gonna take the bait.

Forget fantasyland, get off that ride
and lose those stupid lame-o slides.
Capitalist tool, I gotta holler:
life here ain't bought with no mickey dollars

See the brothers smokin' crack in the dark
hallways of buildings everyone forgot.
Sistas workin' tables in skimpy clothes;
too many shifts for a few lonely blows.

Watch abuela mugged for two fifty-nine
as the 6 reaches the end of the line.
Hear the cold steampipes screeching for some slack.
Feel the sweat running tracks down your tired back.

Come out here, take a walk in my sneakers,
and cast your eyes on these sorry teachers,
spinnin' what they say is our history.
But why we missin' is the mystery.

The door slams shut on my old man's hard day.
His coño drops like a puta's last lay.
On TV some creep talks about a loan
to buy dreams we ain't never gonna own.

Man, this ain't the happiest place up here.
There is no money for no souvenirs.
No fairy is coming down from the moon —
just cause you preachin' statehood's coming soon —

to turn your hair blond and straight, your eyes blue
since you visited some dude's dream come true.
Shit, don't reach for that fifty-first star yet.
Don't think it's all set, don't put down a bet.

'Cause soon everyone will know it, goddam,
That America ain't no Disneyland.

Walking the Ghetto With Miguel and Piri

For me the South Bronx
was not a jungle
populated by pimps and junkies.
Nor some uncivilized outpost
in the urban wild west
where killing was the people's
main goal in life.

I think this walking along
with Miguel and Piri,
trying to recognize
beyond their graffiti
images of my ghetto.

A mental wasteland,
dreams deferred
on the way to the bodega.
My body clothed,
my stomach filled,
the home nuclear,
memories clear the hovering haze.

Miguel and Piri,
addiction to sports our only jones;
lingering into sweaty nights,
singing to Led Zeppelin and Al Green
as the basketball bounced
hypnotically against the asphalt.

The leaves fell,
the first kick-off,
school started and I
ran to buy supplies
at the five and dime.
Eggs-smeared windows,

chalk-slinging socks;
pernil, arroz con gandules
to celebrate our thanks.

Sledding winterland at St. Mary's,
zooming down on a refrigerator door,
snowball fights, laughter in icy darkness,
slow-mo football in the snow.
Christmas lights brightened fire escapes.

Vining for Easter,
bumpin' and grindin' to tunes.
Copping a kiss and a feel,
covering hard-ons with books
on the subway,
checking myself in the mirror,
wondering if girls think I'm cute.

My drugs were books.
Trekked to the library a mile away
for a fix, farther for the *Times*.
Cultural deprivation they say:
no museums,
no Mozart.

After the museums,
Mozart, the degrees,
I meet Miguel and Piri,
listen to their stories,
searching for the way back.
From a distance I sense
pain zig-zagging down the street,
none of us any closer to home.

Departures

Concrete ended in St. Mary's Park
and escape cultivated green
over hills turned to mountains,
trees harboring monsters, along pathways
snaking to battlefields, icy fortresses,
islands hiding pirates burying treasure,
whenever sneakers lifted from asphalt.

The plane sputtered into that space
we shared; the pilot seeking refuge
among children in football gear,
our coach's words engulfed
by rattling propellers
now groaning with desperation.

Quique clutched my shoulder, grounding me
as the herd charged toward smoke.
Outside the supermarket, when he heard
the crash, he said "Luisito,"
and took off, left mami praying curbside.
I looked up at my brother's strained eyebrows,
shut lips. I wanted to see the wreckage.
"Let's go" is all he said.

Now, tucked away in a home,
he hobbles on plastic leg, his mind
coasting to places dulled by drugs
muting those cloudy voices in white,
beating him into silence.

Bronx Aubade
for Lee

Your sturdy steps to the bathroom
announced the coming dawn.
You would leave,
> before the salseros broke night,
> before the neighbor's alarm radio
>> set Frankie Crocker off
> before the kids would clomp
>> to school with their backpacks.
The streetlamp outside cast a glow on your face.
Your perfume stoked my imagination,
and your eyes beckoned
even as they dismissed me:
> My parents, you explained.

While you pressed the red dress
that had captivated me all night,
like a bull under a matador's spell,
I threw glances at you hoping
that you would stay.
But the iron rolled on,
your eyes set on the creases.

Your high heels clacked
towards the chugging taxi,
the only noise breaking
the Bronx air, until
the slamming of the car door.

You left,
the wrinkles in the bed still warm;
but now I understand your silence,
how it spoke to the labor of love
and the simplicity of its method.

Exotic Cuisine

"I've never had Latin"
she whispered in his ear
as she undressed him
removing layers
like slivers off a mango.

Pink nipples, centered
on blue-veined breasts,
last thing he saw
before his face slammed
into perfumed blond hair.

Long, pale legs, swerving
while bracelets branded his neck
and guttural moans, emanating
from some deep dark corner,
grew into screams that rocked him.

Through blurry eyes he saw
her distant smile change
to sated laughter, leaving him
outside his skin, an unwitting voyeur.

She would return to re-live the scene,
spark the fantasy by again melting
into what she called bedroom eyes.
A drowning macho
jumping into limpid pools,
his heart uneasy,
stomach nauseous,
as he grows hard again.

BiWays

You hinge on the borders of desire,
a chronic craving for the Other's touch.

Your tongue waits for instruction
while your life runs like a subtitled film.

As you observe that even the most secluded
roads always offer at least two options,

you entertain following the brighter star
but set the compass for another direction.

Reversing your tracks you return to revel
again and again in suspended pandemonium,

until the moving faces reveal to you
the location of this nothingness with a name.

Rather than stressing on these complexities
you come to see the ride is the thing.

This ride along the enduring jagged highway
that provides the response to blending inertia.

Indeed, the ride, the quintessential thing,
that a simple line cannot divide or blur.

Danny

Danny had the Ché look down.
Cradled in his heart the poet's fire.
From some waspy prep to the fancy private college
he came carrying Rican dreams built on clouds.

That gun a pardon
from the sentence he imposed.
More than tissue and bone he broke
the hand that holds creation's promise.

Danny, the preacher's son
who became the white girl's drug.
Danny, the mystic MIA
with the manic laugh infecting you with life.
Danny with cigarette scars on his body and mind.

Ballads & Boleros

In my teens
coming home,
an Irish ballad streamed
from the corner bar,
made me stop, listen
to music and words
until a drunken tenor
soloed,
"Get outta here, spic."

Today a Chieftains tune
holds me. The lyrics blend
into boleros, laughter embracing
the blood and broken bodies.
The notes seeking refuge,
return me to that echo.

If we could meet again,
I'd ask him to join me
in a duet. To drink
to yesterdays, sing
unchained melodies,
until our throats croak
sunlight into empty glasses.

Snake in the Snow

Skin hides like a snake in snow.
It bites me right between the eyes.
While pneumatic coats devour lean thighs,
scarves mask-tape moist lips;
rubber boots stomp popsicle toes.
As icicled air flattens perfumed roundness,
the whistling freezes my mind.

Sand licked my sun-burnt body
and ocean waves rode my loins.
I had never French kissed,
had never chiki chiki on a jazzy night.
And the snake escaped the snow.

Life is a beach proclaim
frigid purveyors of Nordic wisdom
who sink afloat frozen islands
where I merengue to the Ice Queen's bolero.
Luisito reveled in that first snowfall,
and frost draped his threadbare soul.
I must undress him to keep him alive.

El sol no se puede tapar con la mano—
though clouds bring hosannas in chorus,
giving the snake more cover to hide.

Speechless in Carajo* County

Like fish and loaves,
history should feed the faithful.
Anger should raise the dead,
make you march up mountains,
come down a guerrillero
before the last Spanish word
falls from your tongue.
Patria should resonate,
in your ears with the passion
of your mother's hot breath
whispering, "Dios te bendiga."

But riding minivan bliss,
Island memories ebb like ocean,
foaming over the call in a wind
that doesn't entrust your ashes
to birds flying south for winter.

The seasons spin, leave you slouching
on your knees, breathless, your voice
blank as lake water on calm nights,
when children's dreams meld
like icicles into snow banks,
lost amid hunkering totems of eyes
blind with white light.

What's left
but to sleep on this muted bed
of broken twigs and peat moss?

*According to the Urban Dictionary "the lookout basket in the top mast of a Spanish galleon ship. Sailors would get very sea sick when assigned to this post, so when they would think of becoming mutinous, the captain would send them up to the carajo as punishment." So it can mean a far and remote place but it has multiple meanings including "get out of here, go fly a kite, go fuck yourself, etc..."

Dreaming With Teeth

A toothache strolls the beach alone.
Incisors fall like kernels off cobs.
Toothless grins dancing in a black hole.
Dentures drowning in expectations.
One abandoned cusped, crying
at the happy ending.

Such visionary morsels augur death,
says Puerto Rican folklore.

In the shadowy world of REM,
dentist becomes Grim Reaper,
this hygienist scraping away,
would be Charon, rowing sternly.
Receding gums, she explains.
Bones once scaffolding monuments
to hungry ambition, now strain,
like air holding drunken trees, waiting.
Sworn to use a water pik, floss more,
gingivitis controlled, I'm dismissed.
To wander among sleepwalkers
pondering holes containing pain,
and the finality of cavities.

To White Editors

I tire of writing as a Puerto Rican
for Puerto Ricans about Puerto Ricans
living Puerto Rican situations
where Puerto Ricans are conflicted,
being Puerto Ricans trapped in settings
only Puerto Ricans could imagine.

Have you ever considered,
I too marvel at the spider's work
and dance around love's mysteries?
That I'm moved by the softness of a child's hand
on my cheek as he stares into my eyes?
Like you I shake my head to see
the collected bodies at the foot of cathedrals
even as I long to share with all who traverse
everything the sun has touched.

But you sit in your white room,
hurling pencils at the ceiling.
"Just do it," you say.

Lucky you,
who never had to evolve
into an "Other,"
to fashion a life not your own.

Madre(Patria)

You're bent over the stove,
white flecks of cloth spot your body.
You came straight from the factory
to prepare yet another meal.
The tyranny of routine
moving your hands along.

I also see you,
hunched over sewing machine,
sacks of piecework crowd
the apartment hiding your sweaty face.

I hear your sobs that rare Christmas Eve
when liquor touched your lips.
The reason unimportant, the pain
as common as the recipe for the coquito
that overwhelmed you.

Work and pain have come to shroud
your life, whether Here or There,
filling the void like ugly ratty chairs.
The past abandoned, other players gone,
you remain standing, hands nimble enough
to knit together the sadness
called our history.

But you do not understand this.
So I must leave you to survive
the suffering that consumes you,
like the unexplainable loss of a child;
absent-minded ritual shaping
our lives, this proud masochism
has left us all blind.

My Son Plays Piano at My Alma Mater

Across the carpeted, furnished parlor,
you play the piano, a piece you composed
after teaching yourself to play.

How would you know, son,
decades earlier my hands roamed keys
groping for chords and harmony
in a similar room on this campus.
Desire so strong to create, my coarse
hands stumbled along my discord.
People passed, their smirks saying
'doesn't that fool know he can't play?'

Today on this cool September evening,
your melody reaches damp corners,
a gloomy walker on solitary paths
somewhere else on the college grounds.
Your hands grace across the handsome instrument
that so long ago seemed like fancy furniture.

"It needs more work," you say.
For me, sitting there gray-haired in the shadows,
it's a magnum opus, a finished symphony.

Later that year, we would visit you again,
to pick you up after that call, the one
that made me hold my breath in fear.
We gathered your belongings,
yelled in the car. And we rode back,
our heated silence streaming
with the music on the radio.

PART II: ALLÁ / HERE

...their lives hanging from the hooks
of the question marks ¿allá? ¿acá?

— Luis Rafael Sanchez, *The Flying Bus*

Bruma

Mysterious, your gauzy dance
dervishing over mountains
mambo stepping through valleys
White hair flowing
cottony robe trailing
Blinding grace
in thickening flight
You are natural
You are dangerous
You are wild and free

To Luis Muñoz Marín

Pan, Tierra y Libertad (Bread, Land and Liberty)
Motto of the Popular Democratic Party

The bread you left us
tastes stale and brittle
in our twisted tongues.

It cannot sustain our desires
and even as our stomachs fill
our souls crave more.

Your cacique heart grabbed the attention
of the jíbaros who understood courage,
and they followed as you knew they would.

But when the moment came,
you turned to them for The Answer,
and hid behind their fear.

You have joined the fortunate
Ricans transcending the limbo state,
falling into permanence.

While we, surviving, still wait
for the coming of another messiah
to tell us what we refuse to hear.

Carimbo
In Memory of Tato Laviera

Brand iron the Spaniards used
to mark the African slaves

Y la Miss Puerto Rico says:
this island burns
with the mark of the carimbo.
Its mark reigns deeper
than the skin.
Who would know it
by looking at me?

I. The Suffering Ships Come
The suffering ships came to these shores
on fruitless quests that planted the seeds.

Bozal, on your strong back
they placed asientos,
said you were of poor spirit
and little strength, but after they worked
the Taínos to death, you tended their fields,
our land, harvested cane, filled
our blood with sweet melao.

Before sunrise they woke you
from the rags serving as a bed.
They marched you to the fields,
fed you food that is now heritage:
Sancocho, funche, surullos, vianda y bacalao.
For you, the food of oppression.
You toiled under the sun and
the ever-present Juan Caliente,
whip with seven tongues, unforgiving
even to those who fell exhausted
between the cane stalks.

To the rhythm of machete blows you took shots
of ron caña to numb the pain, to forget
the number of days since leaving home.
With the women you worked
and cursed in song the mayordomo,
who squeezed life out of you,
working you at a pace not fit for beasts.

II. The Carimbo At Work
When the new ones arrived,
hands caressed faces and shoulders.
Those branded, feeling what they
would never see in a mirror,
scarred tissue, homecoming
to the New World, door
to fading memories.

They got a few hours of rest
to watch, to re-live again and again
the carimbo do its work.
Whether shoulder or face
depended on the mayordomo's mood.
Pity the poor devil with defiant gaze.
The young woman selected for his bed
they stripped to the waist,
fondling her breasts as hot metal
came down on her backside.

Forced to recall, grasping to forget,
burnt flesh filled their nostrils.
Screams crowded the little space
they occupied under the heavy sun.
As rolling lisps bounced
along waves of laughter
and talk turned to mundane things,
the one holding the brand iron

marveled at how well black skin heals
before bringing out the children.

At night the worm-like scar swelled
and undulated across a shiny sea
going nowhere, but even the breeze
would not soothe its delirious pace.

III. Ecce Boricua
In the gallego's heart sang the moor
when passion moved him there,
to take what he thought he owned.

Así nació el boricua
En una cama de caña
Under a starlit canopy
Balmy breeze for sheets

We do not call her Malinche.
But mujer caribeña, madre.
Her scream a roar of survival
crowning a people
connected to the sun.
She started our pulse beating to clave.
Fed us milk that became café con leche.
Filled our veins with strength,
stuffed our tongues
with the language of plena.

Asi nacio el boricua, negrito,
En una cuna de caña, riqueña

IV. Coro
We march in fine line
through the constant in-between.
This mulatto nation that doesn't know
where black ends and white begins.

Living in common ground too long
they search revealing signs,
in growing things they take for dying.
Outing others from the race closet.
Pointing to la taja they try to hide.

                              La prueba del abanico
Y tu abuela dónde está?
                              If I listened to these folks
                              Everyday be a bad-hair day
        You say negrito means love,
        but you say it only when
        you order me around

                 We don't need no stinkin' hyphen
                 'cause we be livin' on the colorline

                              The rainbow people
No soy negro, soy indio

The missi says: No se habla de cosas delicadas,
                 como de raza, thank you
                 It's understood we're all fucked up

                              In the whitest of the Antilles

Stop looking for blue eyes
In mine you will only find yourself

                              Don't call me trigueño
                              Can't you see how
                              I dissolve into night?

Un negro perfilao
Negro, pero buena gente

V. Where are you going, Cimarrón?

You escaped your amo,
ran into the hills with armed men
in pursuit. I am ashamed
your defiance has come to this.
With Toño Chauboniel you proclaimed
"more blood will flow than Haiti."
You rebelled in haciendas,
You rebelled in streets,
you fought for freedom,
your passion blinding you
to Holstein's false promises.

You would run and run knowing
all roads always led to water.
And if they caught you
el cepo would greet you,
your wrists and neck locked for days.
But you would rise again and run and run.

Look around now, see how your people
brandish chains and call them jewelry.
Armed foreigners called guests
bomb and kill our people; these
are accidents, oppression
proclaimed free association.
I would tell you to stop your flight.
Don't waste your time.
Your descendents deserted themselves
to enslave each other
for MacDonald's and cupones.
But your spirit must live.
It must live like an ember
to a man on a cold night,
forever burning like Juan's cross
glowing down the stark river.

VI. Condembé
Adombé, ganga, mondé

Let the condembé begin.
Invite all my relatives
European, African and Taíno.
Bomba and plena will play 'til dawn.
Ñam-ñam, Calalú y quimbombó,
mondongo, ananá, and gandinga.
The feast unfolds and we
nourish our blackness.

Tutún de pasa y grifería
Pales and Laviera will be there.
So will Campeche, Schomburg,
Clemente and El Canario.
Ruth Fernández, Juan Boria,
and Rafael Hernández, too.
El Gran Cocoroco will sing.
La Gran Cocoroca will dance.

In Loiza the vejigantes rock
to the rhythms of Obatalá.
Let music lift you
from this island to the other
where boricuas hip hop
to the trú cu tu
trú cu tu
pra pra pra
boogaloo,
calabó
y bamboo.
La sangre llama
la llama sangra.

How this blood surges
like a mighty river through our veins.

It is Tembandumba's gift to us.
Open the floodgates.
Let it run, let it wash the streets.
Let it drown babilongo.
Put a fufú on those who
deny the grifería in our hearts.
Si no tiene dinga, tiene mandinga.

Yoruba congas and bongoces move feet
in Manhattan nightclubs, spill salsa
onto sidewalks from boom boxes.
They arouse tropical winds
and melt frigid city air,
as the arpón calls us to respond
to history in the colors
of calabo, cafole, caoba.

Clave keeps us on a course
as strong as Langston's rivers.
We wait for Oggun's protection,
and let Yemaya bring us home.

So come with me
into the night
to free abuela,
to let her take flight
into the light of the dark.
Come, listen to the bata.
Surrender to the danza negra.

Legacy

I see the Pava flag waving.
Tearful men yell fuego popular,
and I am frightened.
The rain taps the tin roof;
serenades me back to sleep.
Mama Julia's eyes console me behind
thick glasses and beer-soaked sighs.
Tío's rocking leg is my horse.
I ride it till sundown before
red clay gobbles up my tiny legs.
Everyone laughs when I speak
make-believe English right before
the plane cranks its four propellers.
I see them whirl,
blur everything but what remains,
a trail of mist and rain.

Doña Vista Talks Suitcases

Seen those no better than cardboard tied with rope to fancy
ones with super wheels. They're all the same. Sad. Today, it's
missi there, come from Las Marias or some other hick town. To
live with Aunt Lolin, or cousin Chuchi, who's happy to see them
for a few months, but then it's "when you gonna move your ass
out?" Which ain't easy, working the same job as Aunt Lolin or
Cousin Chuchi. Used to be some sweatshop don't care if you're
American—paid you as illegal. Even college kids 'cause they
don't know English. Nowadays, ain't many sweatshops—so it's
flippin' burgers, cleanin' toilets, servin' cafeteria food to bunch a
brats. Same difference; takes forever to save money to move into
another crappy apartment. Seen so many suitcases in my day. I
feel sorry for dem— listen, I was greener than a guayaba. Didn't
know shit. That's why I get sad when I see their bags—Comin'
or goin,' don't matter. It's someone died, or la nena or el nene's
got problems —know what I mean? The lucky ones—they done
with this place; smart ones saved and bought a house in PR.
And then the ones that don't got a dime but gotta return any-
ways 'cause they can't take it no more. All of dem, it's like they
carryin dreams in dem suitcases, and no matter where they goin'
they ain't got no place to park their dreams.

Abuela

Light-skinned, thin lips,
and blond hair, so they say.
Mejoraste la raza?
Puerto Rico will never know.
The answer tucked in stained sheets
like a bendición that echoes,
a lullaby without words.

Consumption took
your image
like your breath,
a blurred old photo
gasping through a story,
unable to finish,
the face lost in the wrinkles,
swept away in time.

DiaspoRican Blues in Black & White
In Memory of Pedro Pietri

I have seen the pictures,
dislocated faces with distant smiles.
Faces that have lost contours of hope,
attentive to the next command,
uprooted from the past.
Fearful of the future, banished from the present,
their eyes hunger for the world.
They've witnessed enough to know
they will not inherit the Earth,
but their lips parch from praying.
I've seen the pictures.

> *Juan left to escape another day without shoes*
> *Miguel left to escape another day of carpetas*
> *Olga left to escape another day of eating pana*

Left with rope-tied suitcases,
recycled from relatives who returned
from their tour of duty chasing dreams.
Dressed as if headed for a grand ball
rather than barrios, fruit farms and factories.
Women in billowy dresses, hats and gloves,
holding babies, the arms of frightened children.
Men in suits and ties, fedora hats, sporting
pencil-thin moustaches and slicked back hair.
Posing at the airport, dwarfed by the plane.

> *Juan left because his love for Luisa would kill him*
> *Miguel left because María's husband would kill him*
> *Olga left because she thought the boredom would kill her.*

My father left with them,
a small-time politician
who spread illusions and seed alike

in the time of the bohemios.
Dressed in white linen suits,
lurking behind cigarette smoke
and greeting card verses, he answered

the harpies' call and the ocean
claimed another restless lover,
an exile without a cause.

My mother followed.
A motherless child,
she passed from one relative
to another, cooking meals for colonels,
cleaning and sewing
while writing her history
on every grain of rice,
every shirt she pressed
at the factory, manufacturing city
dreams found in black & white magazines.

The bloodline infected with wanderlust
calls me too, the past eludes me
even here on this island,
where the earth cradles its monuments.
The roots don't mend or anchor
and I'm cast adrift again to where
the wind blows and the seeds drop.

Pitiyanqui
(from petite yankee)

At sixteen,
I rode the winding road
that hugged mountains,
before the autopista,
to return to the land of my birth.

Local boys greeted me
by branding me pitiyanqui.
Mocked my clothes,
how I spoke Spanish,
said all Nuyoricans were
drug addicts on welfare,
gave real Puerto Ricans
a bad name, that I could never be
boricua.

I responded with fists,
and returned to my aunt's house,
pilgrim soul and body bruised.
At night my muted sobs
accompanied the singing coquís
while I counted the days left
to leave this foreign land;
to where I would return years later
to hear kids call my son a gringo
for speaking English in the schoolyard.

Letrina

The strange white apparatus
with the always gaping mouth
squatted in that hard-walled room.

My uncle told me
from the depth of the bowl
a hand would rise and wipe me clean.
I believed him and remained
constipated longer than I care to recall
that first week in America.

Years later
visiting the island as a Nuyorican,
I encountered the latrine outside
my aunt's house at an urgent moment.
Peering into the dark hole below,
desire was lost amid the stench.
Mosquitoes welcomed my flesh,
offering marked blood
before this dank temple where light
rays splintering through cracks
leave you in gloaming silence.

Post Office, Borinquen, U.S.A.

An old woman rants
about a letter from her soldier son.
She goes on and on, talking to the walls.

No one dares speak or give her eyes a sign,
like in abuelo days when a shoulder
grab cost nothing and smiles could melt icebergs.

The clerk tells her to move along,
line shuffles to buy postage.
No one notices when they slap
stamps on her forehead,
and send her to the seniors' home.

End of route; no forwarding address,
unregistered, not certified, COD not required.

Nothing Washes to the Sea

Morning starts in rage
at rain, the end of a weekend,
a town navigating a day.

Anger builds
between the mundane and
yearning with nowhere to go.

In the classroom, no refuge;
words meant to transform
repaid with cutting digital beeps.

Rain continues, brooding
into her brain, spilling everywhere,
washing nothing to the sea.

At home, no shelter.
Junk mail, Claridad for supper,
a prelude to this muddled quest.

Night catches her, smoldering,
quartered in a full size bed,
the heart still an island.

The Crux

These crosses along the road
stake out final claims
of men rushing to smash a face.
Their legs heavy, the tires free
them on a binge to find answers
in cement and gravel.

Those crosses that sprout along the lawn,
merge into a blinding white mass.
Blood money for frequent flyer miles,
lives sacrificed on foreign altars,
buried before picking up a rifle.
The island's somber migration
that leaves us lingering for answers.

The students pencil crosses
on their exams to light
the way for success; instead they
will carry them across the pond,
and back again, their belts tightened;
or they will place them alongside
shattered glass or near the casket,
or raise them like tenements in cities
where they will taste vinegar,
and weep for their children.

Taíno Trance

I cannot see you Y'ay'a
but your presence fills my body
like sacred powder entering
caverns into my spirit
cleansing releasing impurities
to feel your eyes on me.

I will not present myself to you
rivers tracking my face.
The terns we follow to the sea
thick with fish, the conch
strewn on the shore
or the shells painting sand
jicotea eggs buried like treasure,
crabs running from the seashore rain.
The colors you wave across the sky.
Great Essence we thank you
for all this and more.
The secrets you whisper to us.
The Tree of Life through which Yaya' speaks.
Wu'a! I will not desecrate this bond.
Give me then a path.

Why do You look down away from my eyes?
Is there sunlight in what you hold?
Magic to stay these intruders
men who turn like shrimp under sun
noise rumbling from their mouths
that numbs our senses.

My words drop before you
like rain into sea.
Once alone in borikén this land
embraced by blue waters now
you send other people to our yucaké.

And I see you caress between your hands
what invaders hold when their lips
flutter quiet like a butterfly.

Oh Grand Master
of all things blessed
do you abandon us
in favor of these sunless hordes?

A Trail in the Rain Forest

Along the trampled trail we've chosen,
the only one we can handle,
dew bends the bromelaids
growing reckless in El Yunque,
"The only tropical rainforest in the US."
Where are the animals? my six-year-old asks.
Only small tree frogs, insects, lizards
scamper through the exotic plants
whose names I'll never know.

We walk past the graffiti,
modern hieroglyphics sprayed on rocks.
Pieces of paper, scatter like the birds
we try to spot, but they're hiding today
among the giant trees with heavy shoulders,
behind leaves wide as skirts that embrace us.

They say you can see a Taíno's face in the rock,
questioning towards the heavens, petrified.
Before us, he worshipped spirits
who would not see the fauna contained,
understood an urgency unknown to us.
We can no longer hear the forest's whispers,
or see through the forest of clouds.

The trail comes full circle to where we started;
faded, as the Taíno face we struggle to reclaim
among the shale, against the green, bubbling canopy.

Survival Plan

To live in Puerto Rico
you need a survival plan
El Departamento de Ay Bendito
recommends one from below:

The Armageddon Plan
Embrace the worst and wait.
Stock supplies from the mega retailers
populating every corner of the island.
Buy a generator, a water tank for your roof.
Worship concrete and urban sprawl.
Accept corruption as a necessary evil.
Find comfort in screeching evangelists.
When you pay taxes, thank the Lord
for humbling you to render onto Caesar.

The Hedonist Plan
Celebrate hurricanes with parties.
Take days off before and after
the world record number of holidays.
Consider car jackings an adventure.
Live out animal fantasies behind rejas.
Overdose on island television.
Find pleasure in the misery of Dominicans.
Make Plaza Las Americas your second home.
Drive on shoulders & concrete dividers;
wave to fellow motorists as you do.

The Ostrich Plan
Stick your head in the sand,
(Viable; you live on a tropical island)
If too impatient to reach a beach,
honor the proverbial and tuck it up your butt instead.
Do not read crime statistics or any social metric.
Do not follow politics.

Ignore unemployment figures.
Ignore cars passing on the shoulders & concrete dividers.
Worship insularismo.
Consider driving over crater potholes like a Disney ride.
Keep chanting "This is the best of two worlds."

On Seeing Frade's "El Pan Nuestro"

Jíbaro, man of the earth,
you bring in your hands
a racimo of struggle and sorrow.
You descend from the light,
barefoot down the hill
to feed your family;
your pava cannot shield
the humility in your eyes
only poverty can paint.

In your afterglow, I burn.
Suspended from history and place,
a Nuyorican stands before you,
drawn to your image,
cursed to understand so well.
To see more than your creator
decades ago in the campos of Cayey:

Glory to the passive,
sanctified in land theirs, yet not;
strength born from weakness,
fingers clutching hope,
like a newborn exposed to light.

21

More than the buildings in Pittsburgh,
the cold so foreign to the tropical
heat on your brown body.
More painful than leaving family
to come to a distant land alone.
How shocking that day they outed
your Africanness.
They didn't understand
you were Puerto Rican.
You didn't understand
the hate lurking behind their stares,
the arrogance in each gesture
meant to put you in your place.
You tried to explain the difference
of being *un negro puertorriqueño,*
as you sat eating on the bus
while your white teammates ate at the hotel;
while the hicks in PA called you nigger
and the blacks called you uppity,
and everyone made fun of your English.

Roberto, our God of Confusion.
We look to you and forget
genetics and history.
We put you on an altar
of ignorance.
We learned nothing from your
18 years in the desert, nothing
from you burdening our cross,
nothing from your transformation
into a black man.

Luna Caribeña

She's wearing an evening dress,
fluttering in the April wind,
spike heels sink into beach sand.
His jacket matches the sterling orb
that suspends ocular against onyx sky.
Tropical heat, bewitching woman,
inviting laughter from red lips.
His desire is resistance—
But the waves tango, a breeze croons.
She clutches forearm for balance.
He swoops closer, music
rippling from the hotel lounge.
They sway in rain, wet clothes
hugging lithe bodies.
The ocean, their dance floor;
their spotlight, the moon.

Culebra

We reunited in that islet
with the Spanish name for snake.
We crossed it several times, hands held
like old lovers abandoned in comfort.
Past the shack that served as courthouse,
the plaza with one solitary bench,
a few palm trees pregnant with coconuts.
On the way to the beach we drove by
a crashed plane standing like a monument.

How easy to recover
the thread, reclaim grace
slipping into every crease
and beauty mark caressed
by hungry fingers and tongues.
Our bodies, supple and toned to the task.

Once embarrassed to make sounds behind
the curtain serving as bathroom door,
now you talk to me, door wide open.
You bristle at my bad habits, lose patience
when I don't listen to your nagging.
We both stir the ashes of our wreckage,
looking for the black box.

There's no sin in wisdom gained.
Nothing ever lost in paradise.
Intimacy just sheds its feet
licks its wounds
and slithers
in the shadows.

Lilo Returns

Se muere Lilo
his dying wish is
to be buried in Tierra Boricua.

The winters bleached his face,
gradually burrowed into his bones.
He earned the Almighty Dollar
to buy a house in a Latino section
of Jersey.
Worked his entire life
for the security of remaining a spic.
Raised children in the mainland
to forget their history.

The last years bed-ridden
a once imposing macho drooling,
unable to control bodily functions
mumbles of resting in the homeland.

Another prodigal son,
Lilo returns to the Patria
in a coffin.
Transported in the underbelly of a jet plane
cargo for worms.
His final offering,
bitter seed for Puerto Rican soil.

Father(Land)

Like Hamlet's ghost you come
to stir twilight in this, your land,
which you left mami to create
in my mind with her memories.

Moments when our paths converge.
tableaux popping along my life,
stations of pain and passion,
a cross I bore for the privilege
of carrying your name.

Él es tu padre, mami reminded,
casting your shadow on my world.
You deserved respect she said
for engendering me
into this terrain, where I'm grounded
rootless, the ocean having separated
more than physical dimensions;
this patria misknown and undefined
also demands what is hard to give.

Doña Vista on Revolúshun

There he go again. Standing on da milk crate wearin' dem army pants and Ché tee shirt, talking about revolúshun, passin' paper nobody gonna read. Coprations this, colonisashun that, ten dollar words, but I'm just seein' anger and hate spittin' outa his mouth. Lots of vinegar, y no hay azúcar. Who he shoutin' at, anyways? Like violence gonna save us. He da War Jesus. He gonna do a revolúshun all by hisself. Ay bendito, learn to love, manito, get yourself kids and see if you wanna talk revolúshun. Talk to your abuelitos about revolúshun. Your words make me feel like I'm back in time, alone on some island that ain't Puerto Rico. Make me feel scared for the future, make me wanna run away, make me wanna jump off this building. M'hijo, this ain't no way to bring your people together.

Ode to Extinction

In the museum of Natural History
a sign reads "The World in a Thousand Years."
Below, a stationary globe invites
attention, a glance at least.
My heart sinks
into the Caribbean Sea.
Puerto Rico is nowhere;
the home(is)land will disappear.
All things shift, while time blinks.
So, Boricuas, let's drift united
into oblivion; we'll celebrate
this fortune along with Columbus,
and hurricanes, ELA; the remaining millennium
as a colony, we'll mambo to climate change,
or praise Jesus, for delivering us
from the evils of decision.

Piropos for the Island from a Nuyorican
A found poem

If your terrain were a jail
and your people chains,
what a beautiful place
to fulfill my sentence.

I'd like to be the sea
to your beach, because then
with the rising of the waves,
I'd touch you from afar.

I want to be a raindrop
falling on your mountains;
to be born in your clouds
fly through your skin and die
in your soil.

From the heavens fell a poet to write
about you but he couldn't find enough
words for such complex beauty.

What can a poet know of beauty
without ever seeing your beaches,
sunshine and mountains.

Know that I love you too much
but I don't know how to love
you less.

I love you more than my mother—
and I sin to think that she gave
me life and you're taking it.

I love you because I love to love you,
because I always have and I'll never know why.

I dreamt the sun froze, the seas burned
and to dream the impossible: that you loved me.

I lived to know you,
and when I did, I understood
I could not live with you.

Life without you makes no sense
because you own my five senses.

Between you and me
the only bad thing is the air
that separates us.

Our paths separated without
hate or anger but how can I call
you friend—if once I called you a love?

I've thought of you only twice:
when I left and the rest of my life.

How can I forget you?
When I want to forget
I forget about forgetting
and I start to remember.

Having something that reminds me of you
is to admit that I can forget you.

If I could grant you a gift,
I'd give you a mirror
Because after you the realistic thing
is your reflection.

If life would grant me a wish, I would
wish to know you again in a freer world.

Perhaps you're not perfect
but your defects are charming.

Perhaps for the world, you're one place,
but for one person, you are many worlds.

You told me it was easy to love,
and I learned, but then you forgot me
and that I couldn't learn.

But the greatest lesson you taught me,
is whoever doesn't love the impossible
does not know how to love.

Tell them I don't care anymore.
That I don't love you, that I don't
remember you any longer—but never tell
them I said this in writing.

Dictionary for the Tourist

Acá: Here, or towards here, but going nowhere.

Adombé, ganga, mondé: "Now we're going to eat" or "now, we're going to dance." (from Luis Pales Matos' *Tuntún de Pasa y Grif-ería).*

Alcapurria: Plaintain fritter stuffed with meat and cholesterol.

Ay Bendito: Popular Puerto Rican expression expressing either pity, resignation, exasperation or each in equal parts. Similar to "estoy jodido."

Allá: There, or towards there, but going nowhere.

Amo: Master, as in the United States.

Ananá: Pineapple, as in "la piña esta agria."

Arpón: Lead singer in Santeria rituals who chants to the gods.

Asientos: Land grants; literally, the word means "seats."

Así nació el mulato: In that way, the mulatto was born.

Autopista: Popular name of Route 52, the first thruway in Puerto Rico; now, any such highway, soon the entire island.

Babilongo: Evil spirit.

Batá: Hour-glassed African drum used in sacred rituals.

Bendición: Blessing; traditionally, Puerto Ricans ask for a "ben-dición" from parents, elders.

Bohemios: "Bohemians;"libertine men flaunting artistic airs.

Bomba y plena: African influenced Puerto Rican dances.

Bombilla: Bulb. Bombilla food so-called because of the heavy lamps used to keep it warm. For some, Puerto Rican haute   cuisine.

Boogalo: Mix of Afro-Cuban and blues rhythms that flourished in New York City during the 1960's-1970's.

Boria, Juan. Famous Afro-Puerto Rican poet.

Boricua: Indigenous name for inhabitants of the island; native Puerto Rican.

Borikén: Indigenous name for the island of Puerto Rico.

Bozal: Native African, as opposed to those born in the Americas who call themselves "triqueño."

Cacique: Taíno word for "chief" or leader; arrogant político.

Calabó: African wood.

Calalú: Okra (quimbombó) soup or stew "of the saints" (Palés Matos).

Caña Brava...Manglar: Bamboo...mangrove.

Carpetas: Formerly classified files or dossiers maintained by F.B.I. on individuals suspected of subversive activities, especially those involved in pro-independence movement.

Chicharrones de cerdo: Crispy, fried strips of pork; a plate ofheart attack.

Cimarrón: Runaway slave.

Claridad: Leftist newspaper in Puerto Rico that advocates independence for the island.

Campeche, Jose. Nineteenth century Afro-Puerto Rican painter.

Condembé: (Sometimes candombé) dance and feast.

Bruma: Fog.

Con lo que cuenta América: This is what America can depend on.

Coño: In Puerto Rico, "damn." In other Hispanic countries, vagina.

Coquí: A small tree frog, native to Puerto Rico, which makes a sound resembling its onomatopoeic name and drives you crazy.

Coquito: Eggnog made with rum; deceptively innocent.

Cordillera: Range of small mountains in central Puerto Rico.

Coro: African-influenced chorus in salsa, in the tradition of   call and response.

Cuajito: Chopped chicken hearts in sauce. Yum.

Cuchifritos: Various *criollo* (creole) foods, usually fried; fritters. Puerto Rican soul food.

Cupones: Federal government issued food coupons. To some, Puerto Rican Dollars.

Danza: Spanish-influenced, slow ballroom dance for blanquitos.

Danza negra: Literally, "black dance." From title of Palés Matos' poem.

Dios te bendiga: God bless you.

El Canario: (The Canary). Famous singer of plenas.

El cepo: A torture device.

Él es tu padre: He's your father.

El Gran Cocoroco: "Grand Chief;" line alludes to Palés Matos' poem, "Danza Negra."

Ellegua: Yoruba god of the crossroads.

El sol no se puede tapar con la mano: You can't hide the sun with your hand.

En coro: In chorus.

En una cama de caña: In a bed of cane stalks.

Fernández, Ruth. Afro-Puerto Rican Singer and Senator (1919-2012).

Fiambrera: Small, stacked tin pots containing lunch. The type of meal eaten in such pots.

Fría: Beer, served ice cold. The name for beer, as in "Dame una fria."

Fuego popular: Literally, "popular fire"; chant yelled by supporters of PDP upon electoral victories. Rare these days.

Fufú: Spell. Not to be confused with *fukú*, Junot.

Funche: Sweet, cornmeal gruel. Puerto Rican grits, sort of.

Gandinga: Chopped pork gizzards in sauce. Double yum.

Grifería: "Nappy" hair.

Hernández, Rafael. Composer of some of Puerto Rico's most famous songs and melodies.

Holstein, Docoudray: In 1822 attempted to establish Puerto Rican republic, with himself as President. He promised the slaves freedom if they participated in overthrow of government, although his intentions were to keep them enslaved if he accomplished his plan.

Jíbaro: Pre-twentieth century subsistence farmer who, to some, represents the essence of Puerto Ricanness.

Jicotea: Turtle.

La llama sangra: Literally, "the flame bleeds." Llama also means "violent passion."

La prueba del abanico: Literally, "The test of the fan." A test for a person's level of "whiteness;" allegedly used by one of the elite Puerto Rican social clubs as a test for admission. A participant had to stand below a ceiling fan to see the degree to which the air would move his or her hair. The more movement, the "better" the hair, and thus the whiter the person.

La sangre llama: Literally, "the blood calls;" kinfolk are naturally drawn to each other.

La taja: Literally, the slice. That piece of Africa that every Puerto Rican has but many deny.

Laviera, Tato. Contemporary Puerto Rican poet who celebrated African heritage.

Mayordomo: Overseer.

Mejoraste la raza: Literally, "did you improve the race"?

Melao: Molasses-type syrup made from sugarcane sap.

Missi: Spanglish form of "Miss" or "Mrs."

Mondongo: Tripe stew. Not for picky eaters.

Morcilla: Blood sausage. Food which it is best not to know how it's prepared.

Mujer caribeña: Caribbean woman.

Muñoz Marín, Luis. First popularly elected governor of Puerto Rico, from 1944-1960. The architect of the Free Associated State form of government. Still revered in Puerto Rico as an icon.

Negrito: Literally, "little black one," considered by some to be a term of endearment, but really racist.

No pasa – Qué Pasa. Quién pasa? : No one passes. What's happening? Who passes?

Oggun: In Santeria, the warrior God. The Big Kahunka.

Pana: Breadfruit; so accessible was this foodstuff, especiallyduring times of near famine, that Puerto Ricans still refer to a faithful friend as "pana."

Pava: Straw hat worn by jíbaros, subsistence farmers; symbol of Popular Democratic Party.

Pendeja/o: Slang for fool; one who commits pendejadas.

Pinga: Slang for penis.

Piropos: A flowery, poetic compliment. Often given to women-walking alone along the street.

Pitiyanqui: Derogatory name for someone who is exceedingly and obsequiously pro-U.S, e.g., PNP and PDP.

Plena: Puerto Rican, African-based traditional dance.

Prócer: Exalted person, leader; "founding father."

Qué Viva Shangó: Long live Shangó. Yoruba god of thunder and lightning.

Puta: Prostitute, whore. The female version of puto.

Racimo: Bunch, as in bananas.

Relleno de papa: Round potato fritter stuffed with meat.

Rejas: Iron or steel bars installed for security purposes. Typical window treatment in Puerto Rico.

Rumberos: Dancers of rumba. Has nothing to do with rum, although drinking said spirit may contribute to dancing.

Ron caña: Also known as *pitorro*. Moonshine made from sugarcane and other unknown and unidentifiable ingredients.

Sancocho: Stew. Great for rainy days and hangovers.

Schomburg, Arturo Alfonso: Afro-Puerto Rican archivist, writer and historian of Africania. Significant contributor to Harlem Renaissance and virtually unknown to Puerto Ricans.

Se muere Lilo: Lilo is dying.

Si no tiene dinga, tiene mandinga: Popular saying in Puerto Rico, affirming African heritage of everyone. Dinga and Mandinga are two African tribes, so if you're not from one, you're from the other.

Surullos: Fried corn meal sticks.

Taíno: The indigenous people of Puerto Rico whose genetic profile, contrary to popular belief, is not extinct in Puerto Rican population.

Tembandumba: According to Palés Matos, a legendary, Amazon-like African matriarch. Legend has it that she had her son assassinated and then spread his blood over her body to instill fear and valor in her warriors. One badass lady.

Tierra Boricua: Boricua land; Puerto Rico.

Tiempo muerto: Literally, "dead time." In Puerto Rico, referred to time after the sugar cane was harvested. Now, state of affairs in the island.

Toño Chauboniel: Leader of planned Puerto Rican slave uprising.

Trigueño: Wheat colored, refers to skin complexion. A term sometimes used by people in self-denial of their African ancestry.

Tumbao: Fundamental bass-line of Afro-cuban music. More tumbao!

Tuntún de Pasa y Grifería: Title of Luis Palés Matos' collection of poems suggestive of Afro-Puerto Rican vitality and influence.

Trú cu tu (etc.): Onomatopoeic sounds of drums, sort of.

Un negro puertorriqueño: Either "a black Puerto Rican" or "a Puerto Rican Negro."

Vejigantes: Masked revelers at the festival of Loiza Aldea, Puerto Rico.

Vianda y bacalao: Roots and codfish.

Virgen de las Ventanas: Virgin of the Windows. Mostly, gossipy, bored old ladies who look out the window all day.

Wu'a: "No"in Taíno language. And wu'a means wu'a.

Y'ay'a: Great Spirit or The Creator.

Yemaya: In Santería, Goddess of the Seas.

Y no hay azúcar: "And there is no sugar."

¿Y tu abuela, dónde está?: "And your grandmother, where is she?" Refers to hypocrites who will not admit to their African ancestry.

Yucaké: Taíno word for "village."★

ABOUT THE POET

J. L. TORRES is Professor of English at SUNY Plattsburgh, where he teaches both American literature, Latina/o Literatures, and Creative Writing. He has published poetry in journals such as the *Denver Quarterly, the Americas Review, Crab Orchard Review, Bilingual Review, Connecticut Review, Tulane Review, Puerto del Sol,* among others, most of which are in BORICUA PASSPORT. He is the author of *The Family Terrorist and Other Stories* (Arte Público, 2008), and the novel, *The Accidental Native* (Arte Público, 2013). Torres also serves as Editor of the *Saranac Review;* and along with Carmen Haydee Rivera, he is the co-editor of *Writing Off the Hyphen: New Perspectives on the Literature of the Puerto Rican Diaspora*. Visit him at www.JLTorres.net/wp or on Facebook.⊛

OTHER BOOKS BY 2LEAF PRESS

2LEAF PRESS challenges the status quo by publishing alternative fiction, non-fiction, poetry and bilingual works by activists, academics, poets and authors dedicated to diversity and social justice with scholarship that is accessible to the general public. 2LEAF PRESS produces high quality and beautifully produced hardcover, paperback and ebook formats through our series: *2LP Explorations in Diversity, 2LP University Books, 2LP Classics, 2LP Translations, Nuyorican World Series,* and *2LP Current Affairs, Culture & Politics.* Below is a selection of 2LEAF PRESS' published titles.

2LP EXPLORATIONS IN DIVERSITY
Substance of Fire: Gender and Race in the College Classroom
by Claire Millikin
Foreword by R. Joseph Rodríguez, Afterword by Richard Delgado
Contributed material by Riley Blanks, Blake Calhoun, Rox Trujillo

Black Lives Have Always Mattered
A Collection of Essays, Poems, and Personal Narratives
Edited by Abiodun Oyewole

The Beiging of America:
Personal Narratives about Being Mixed Race in the 21st Century
Edited by Cathy J. Schlund-Vials, Sean Frederick Forbes, Tara Betts
with an Afterword by Heidi Durrow

What Does it Mean to be White in America?
Breaking the White Code of Silence, A Collection of Personal Narratives
Edited by Gabrielle David and Sean Frederick Forbes
Introduction by Debby Irving and Afterword by Tara Betts

2LP UNIVERSITY BOOKS
Designs of Blackness, Mappings in the Literature and
Culture of African Americans
A. Robert Lee
20TH ANNIVERSARY EXPANDED EDITION

2LP CLASSICS
Adventures in Black and White
Edited and with a critical introduction by Tara Betts
by Philippa Duke Schuyler

Monsters: Mary Shelley's Frankenstein and Mathilda
by Mary Shelley, edited by Claire Millikin Raymond

2LP TRANSLATIONS
Birds on the Kiswar Tree
by Odi Gonzales, Translated by Lynn Levin
Bilingual: English/Spanish

Incessant Beauty, A Bilingual Anthology
by Ana Rossetti, Edited and Translated by Carmela Ferradáns
Bilingual: English/Spanish

NUYORICAN WORLD SERIES
Our Nuyorican Thing, The Birth of a Self-Made Identity
by Samuel Carrion Diaz, with an Introduction by Urayoán Noel
Bilingual: English/Spanish

Hey Yo! Yo Soy!, 40 Years of Nuyorican Street Poetry,
The Collected Works of Jesús Papoleto Meléndez
Bilingual: English/Spanish

LITERARY NONFICTION
No Vacancy; Homeless Women in Paradise
by Michael Reid

The Beauty of Being, A Collection of Fables, Short Stories & Essays
by Abiodun Oyewole

WHEREABOUTS: Stepping Out of Place,
An Outside in Literary & Travel Magazine Anthology
Edited by Brandi Dawn Henderson

PLAYS
Rivers of Women, The Play
by Shirley Bradley LeFlore, with photographs by Michael J. Bracey

AUTOBIOGRAPHIES/MEMOIRS/BIOGRAPHIES
Trailblazers, Black Women Who Helped Make America Great
American Firsts/American Icons
by Gabrielle David

Mother of Orphans
The True and Curious Story of Irish Alice, A Colored Man's Widow
by Dedria Humphries Barker

Strength of Soul
by Naomi Raquel Enright

Dream of the Water Children:
Memory and Mourning in the Black Pacific
by Fredrick D. Kakinami Cloyd
Foreword by Velina Hasu Houston, Introduction by Gerald Horne
Edited by Karen Chau

The Fourth Moment: Journeys from the Known to the Unknown, A Memoir
by Carole J. Garrison, Introduction by Sarah Willis

POETRY
PAPOLíTICO, Poems of a Political Persuasion
by Jesús Papoleto Meléndez
with an Introduction by Joel Kovel and DeeDee Halleck

Critics of Mystery Marvel, Collected Poems
by Youssef Alaoui, with an Introduction by Laila Halaby

shrimp
by jason vasser-elong, with an Introduction by Michael Castro
The Revlon Slough, New and Selected Poems
by Ray DiZazzo, with an Introduction by Claire Millikin

Written Eye: Visuals/Verse
by A. Robert Lee

A Country Without Borders: Poems and Stories of Kashmir
by Lalita Pandit Hogan, with an Introduction by Frederick Luis Aldama

Branches of the Tree of Life
The Collected Poems of Abiodun Oyewole 1969-2013
by Abiodun Oyewole, edited by Gabrielle David
with an Introduction by Betty J. Dopson

2Leaf Press is an imprint owned and operated by the Intercultural Alliance of Artists & Scholars, Inc. (IAAS), a NY-based nonprofit organization that publishes and promotes multicultural literature.

NEW YORK
www.2leafpress.org